UW HUSKIES *from A to Z*

By Leinora Stuart & Kristi Ascani

Illustrated by Naphtali Morden & Stephan Moss

Rainier Vista looking towards Red Square, UW Campus, 2007.

University of Washington, Seattle, Washington

Established: 1861
Mascot: Husky
Motto: "Lux sit"

Green Beanie Books

Photo Credits:

For A (Joe Sutter): Courtesy Joseph Sutter. For A/Kirsten Wind Tunnel: Courtesy University of Washington Aeronautical Laboratory. For B: Courtesy The Bancroft Library, University of California, Berkeley 308s.B6 1938 v. 65, p. 143. For C (UW2234), E (UW23078), G/Tubby Graves (UW35605), G/Hec Edmundson (UW35606), I (UW35608), J (UW29653z) Photo by Mary Randlett, K (UW2117), L/Meany and Suzzallo (UW2235), N/Young Naturalists (UW21691), O/The Hook (UW28121), P (UW35609), Q/Campus Day (UW20481z), S (Lee 20042) Photo by James P. Lee, T/Denny (UW2829) Bagley (UW27900z) Columns (UW6272), U/Foege (UW356470), Y/Rally (UW21987z) Dobie (UW35607): Courtesy University of Washington Libraries, Special Collections. For D and F: Courtesy Dave Torrell. For G/Lawrie: Courtesy Jesse Beals/JBOriginals. For L/Suzzallo Library, N/Poles, O/Denny Bell, Q/Cherry Trees, R/"Broken Obelisk", and W: Courtesy Leinora Stuart. For M: Walter P. Reuther Library, Wayne State University. For R/Red Square Photo by Johnny Moore: Courtesy University of Washington, University Photography. For U/Quinton: Courtesy of Special Collections, David O. McKay Library, Brigham Young University-Idaho. For V and Title Page: Courtesy Loyd C. Heath, Photography. For X: Courtesy Katherine B. Turner/UW Admissions. For Z/Lubchenco: Courtesy National Oceanic and Atmospheric Administration, Z/Malcom: Courtesy American Association for the Advancement of Science. Photo by: Michael Colella.

Photo Credits for Illustration References:

For A: Courtesy the Boeing Company. For B, D, H, L, N, O, P, Q, R, T, V, Z and Cover: Courtesy Leinora Stuart. For C and F (UW Crew) Photo by Andy Rogers (UW Band) Photo by Scott Eklund: Courtesy Red Box Pictures. For C: Courtesy Max Waugh. For D and Cover: Courtesy Kristi Ascani. For I, K, and S: Courtesy Carla Nellis. For J: Courtesy National Archives. For M: Courtesy Rose Zurek. For W and X: Courtesy Getty Images. For Y: Courtesy Greg Davis Sports Photography.

Author photo by Kerry Carty

Special Permissions: Beverly Cleary book image used with permission from Harper Collins Publishers, Burke photos used with permission from The Burke Museum of Natural History and Culture, Pacific Science Center logo used with permission from the Pacific Science Center, WSU Cougars logo used with permission from Washington State University, Lyrics to Bow Down to Washington, © copyright 1916, Courtesy University of Washington

Green Beanie Books
P.O. Box 7405
Bonney Lake, WA 98391

For more information about our books, visit us online at greenbeaniebooks.com

Printed and bound in the United States

ISBN 978-1-937499-06-8

Library of Congress Control Number: 2013936047

FSC
www.fsc.org
MIX
Paper from responsible sources
FSC® C002589

This book is printed on paper that is acid-free and meets the requirements of the American National Standards Institute for Permanence of Paper for Printed Library Materials, Z39.48-1992.

Green Beanie Books
www.greenbeaniebooks.com

To my Husky-loving family and friends, thank you for all of your support and encouragement; and to all Dawg fans out there, WOOF!

–LS

To my family and partners in crime, many thanks for your encouragement, and cheers to many great seasons to come!

–KA

Author's Note:

As students and friends at the UW years ago, never did we imagine that one day we would have the opportunity to coauthor a heartfelt book about the school that would touch our lives in so many ways. Our hope as Husky alums, as mothers, and as educators is to share the rich history and proud traditions that make the UW so special. Although the 26 letters of the alphabet offer a perfect framework to illustrate this unique view of our school, it was also our greatest challenge. Despite our earnest efforts to tell these stories thoroughly, we have no doubt missed a few nuggets along the way. For this we offer our sincerest apologies and hope that what is included will inspire Husky pride for all current students, alumni, and Huskies yet to be.

Go Dawgs!

-LS and KA

A is for Aeronautics and Astronautics

Talk of Seattle often makes people think of airplanes. The University of Washington has played a key role in putting Seattle on the world map as a city that builds magnificent flying machines.

William E. Boeing came to the area in 1903—the same year the Wright brothers flew the first airplane. He later started the Boeing Airplane Company. His first two employees were UW graduates. This began an amazing partnership between the UW and Boeing that has endured for more than a century. In fact, William Boeing funded the construction of a wind tunnel at the UW for testing wind speed. Because of this, the UW agreed to teach students about aeronautics. Some of the most skilled engineers in the industry have graduated from the UW. In November 2012, the university approved renaming the department the William E. Boeing Department of Aeronautics and Astronautics. William also helped fund the Kirsten Wind Tunnel, named for **Frederick Kirsten**, the first aeronautics professor at the UW. It still operates on the campus and has been used to test some of the greatest airplanes in the past century.

Joseph Sutter is often referred to as the father of the Boeing 747 jumbo jet. Joseph grew up watching airplanes land in Boeing Field and dreamed of designing planes one day. He graduated from the UW in 1943 with a degree in aeronautical engineering. Three years later, the Boeing Airplane Company hired him to design planes. Eventually and against all odds, Joseph led a team of 4,500 people to create the 747, a majestic jet that continues to fly around the globe. Joseph received the Alumnus Summa Laude Dignatus Award in 2001 for his contributions to the field of aeronautics. The award is the highest honor the university bestows on its alumni.

Joe Sutter relaxing on the UW campus.

Thar she blows! Professor Kirsten (right) with a worker inside the Kirsten Wind Tunnel, 1936.

Fast Fact: Creating the world's first jumbo jet, the Boeing 747, was no easy task. The effort involved 75,000 engineering drawings and required more than ten million hours of labor. Husky legend, Joseph Sutter, led his team to design the amazing flying machine in less than three years. The project was launched in March 1966—and the first 747 took flight on February 9, 1969.

From Joseph's mind, with pen and pad,
Came sketches from this Husky lad.
With fortitude he led his team
To build this jumbo flying dream!

B is for **Beverly Cleary**

Does the name *Ribsy* or *Ramona Quimby* bring a smile to your face? If so, you're among the millions of young readers who devoured stories about these funny characters written by beloved author and UW graduate **Beverly Cleary**. Her books have won numerous awards, including one Newbery Medal and two Newbery Honors. Beverly grew up on a farm in Yamhill, Oregon. She was an only child who loved having her mother read to her from the two books Beverly owned. When Beverly was five years old, her mother started a library because there wasn't one in their town. Beverly at last had new stories to read.

When Beverly was in third grade, a newspaper club offered a free book to students who wrote a book review. Because her mother often encouraged her to "try," Beverly did just that and wrote her first piece. The newspaper published her picture along with her review. In seventh grade, Beverly wrote a story about a girl who met Beverly's favorite storybook characters in a place called Bookland. After reading the story, Beverly's teacher encouraged her to continue writing—and to consider writing children's books someday.

Determined to become a librarian, Beverly studied library and information sciences at the UW. She hoped to work with children. After graduating in 1939 and then working as a librarian, she wrote her first book. Beverly tried to remember the kinds of stories she'd wanted to read as a child. In 1950, she completed *Henry Huggins*, about a third-grade boy and his dog, Ribsy. She was inspired to write stories about characters she would have related to as a child. Since then, Beverly Cleary has won numerous awards. In 2008, the UW honored her with the Alumnus Summa Laude Dignatus Award. Her stories continue to bring joy to readers, both young and old. Named a "Living Legend" by the Library of Congress in 2000, she is certainly a Husky legend, too.

Beverly Cleary at UC Berkeley before attending UW, 1938.

Fast Fact: Because she caught the chicken pox and smallpox in first grade, Beverly had to miss many days of school. She quickly fell behind in her schoolwork, and she became especially nervous about any activity or assignment that involved reading. With the guidance of a patient teacher, Beverly found stories she enjoyed reading. She began to catch up at school and went on to become a world-renowned children's author.

Everyday tales of girls and boys—
A mouse whose cycle made some noise.
Funny kids she wrote about . . .
Beverly, your books we tout!

C is for Crew

Where are you likely to hear shouts including "Let it run!" and "Square on the ready!" and "Oars away!"? There's a good chance you'll hear those colorful phrases—and others—when the UW crew team is racing! The University of Washington rowing team dates back to 1901, and it has been a fan favorite ever since.

With its crew house perched at the edge of Lake Washington, the UW crew seemed destined for greatness. In 1936, **Al Ulbrickson's** eight-man team came from behind to win a gold medal in the Berlin Olympics. Twelve years later, the UW crew again won gold at the London Olympics.

By 1977, the UW women's crew had emerged as a powerful force as well. Five years earlier, Title IX became law, which among other things, meant that women would have equal opportunities in collegiate sports. The UW women's team took the gold medal in the 1984 Olympics in the eight-oared shell event. Over the years, the UW men's and women's rowing teams have continued to win at the highest levels of competition.

The UW crew has had many amazing coaches, rowers, and coxswains over the years. A coxswain (pronounced KOK-suhn) directs the rowers from the stern, encouraging them to row in sync. **Hiram Conibear**, known as the founding father of rowing at the UW, invented a powerful motion that came to be known as the Conibear stroke. Legendary shell builder

George Pocock designed sleek, light racing shells that improved performance. In recent years, coaches **Michael Callahan** and **Bob Ernst** have continued the legacy of greatness for rowing at the UW.

To kick off the boating season each spring, fans line the nearby Montlake Cut for the Windermere Cup regatta. Although it began as a local rowing competition in 1970, the regatta now draws competitors and fans from around the globe.

The unbeatable gold medal champions, 1936 UW Olympic crew team.

Fast Fact: In 1958, the UW men's rowing team was out for revenge. They had been beaten by the Leningrad Trud Rowing Club. Coached by the legendary Al Ubrickson, the team traveled to Moscow—determined to beat the Soviets on their own turf. And beat them they did! Announced by local broadcaster Keith Jackson on KOMO Radio, the event is believed to be the first-ever sporting competition broadcast from behind the Iron Curtain.

The coxswain shouts out to the crew—
"Ready all, row!" And right on cue,
Husky rowers begin to row,
Then pull ahead—go, Huskies, go!

D is for **Dawgs**

"Woof!" If you have ever been to a University of Washington sporting event, you have most likely heard this Husky call. The university's mascot is the Husky dog, which is represented with both a live mascot and a costumed Husky character.

Deciding on a mascot was no simple task for the UW. In 1919, Sunny Boy, a cartoon character in a campus magazine called the Sun Dodgers, struck the students' fancy. They loved the name so much, they began calling their teams the Sun Dodgers. For games, they carried a carved golden statue of Sunny Boy onto the field. The mascot lasted just a few years because too many people were inclined to ask: "What is a Sun Dodger exactly?"

After also trying out the Indians and the Vikings as names, the UW ultimately chose the Alaskan Malamute Husky in 1922 as the official mascot, truly capturing Seattle's legacy as the "gateway to the Alaskan frontier." The malamute is also known as the biggest and the strongest of all Husky breeds.

Born in 2008, **Dubs** is the thirteenth live mascot for the UW. He follows in the paw steps of legendary Husky mascots such as Frosty I, Wasky, King Chinook, Regent Denali, King Redoubt, and Spirit who delighted fans over the years with their distinct personalities and charm.

Originally called the Husky Dog, **Harry the Husky** was introduced as the UW's second mascot in 1995. A human dressed in a husky costume, Harry attends sporting events both on and off campus. Fans know Harry's jersey number is 00, but the identity of the lucky person inside the costume is a secret.

Both Harry and Dubs play important roles in promoting school spirit at the UW. Keep your eyes open for them at the next Husky game—and be sure to bring a camera, as they love to take photos with all Husky fans!

One amazing Dawg! A Husky mascot with cheerleaders at a 1960s-era UW game.

Fast Fact: Frosty I, the UW's first official Husky mascot adopted in 1922, was often found wandering the campus and local neighborhoods. He was known as a friendly dog and went missing so often that a local taxi company took on, free of charge, the responsibility of escorting Frosty home.

"Woof!" goes Dubs's and Harry's shout!
To Husky fans they leave no doubt
Of their spirit and Husky pride.
Dubs and Harry—you're on our side!

E is for Exposition of 1909

The Space Needle rises 604 feet above the city of Seattle. This unique landmark was built for the 1962 World's Fair. However, Seattle has hosted two World's Fairs. The first was in 1909, when the Alaska-Yukon-Pacific Exposition, or A-Y-P, attracted nearly four million people.

At the time, many people still viewed the young city as part of the Wild West. The fair was a chance to show the world that Seattle was a cultured city with plentiful resources and breathtaking beauty. It was also was an opportunity to advance trade among the countries on the Pacific Rim, especially Japan.

Edmond Meany, a UW graduate and state lawmaker, suggested that the A-Y-P be held on the UW campus. He saw the idea as an excellent opportunity to build up the grounds, which is exactly what happened. With funds granted, forests were cleared and buildings were built. Formal gardens were planted and pathways were laid. As Edmond had hoped, the effort benefited the UW in the years that followed.

Air travel was new, and **Bud Mars's** gas-filled airship stole the show at the A-Y-P. Countries and states built pavilions to display their resources and cultures. Sparkling displays of gold nuggets and a life-size elephant made of walnuts thrilled the crowds. But one area of the fair was a crowd favorite—the Pay Streak, which included a Ferris wheel and other rides, international food and Chinese tea, curious sideshows, music,

and parades that drew crowds day and night.

The A-Y-P was held from June 1 to October 16, 1909, and it was a spectacular showcase for Seattle. The fair is sometimes referred to as Exposition Beautiful, but Huskies have reason to think of it fondly as the time "the world came to campus."

Airship pilot, JC "Bud" Mars wowed the crowds with his flight over Geyser Basin at the A-Y-P, 1909.

Fast Fact: In 1908, Henry Ford faced financial ruin, even though his Model T was in production. When the A-Y-P opened on June 1, 1909, an auto race from New York to the UW campus began, with a $2,000 prize. Six courageous racers competed despite few drivable roads, flat tires, muddy trails, and the hazards of Snoqualmie Pass. Ford's Model T came in first place in just twenty-two days. An immediate national marketing blitz catapulted the Model T into automobile history. As it turned out, the car was later disqualified. That bump in the road didn't matter to Henry Ford—he was back in business, thanks to the A-Y-P!

Music, gardens, Ferris wheel,
Chinese tea and rides that thrill.
The world came to A-Y-P
At our university!

F is for **Fight Song**

Sometimes entering a contest just for fun pays off! That's how "Bow Down to Washington" became the University of Washington's official fight song. In 1915, the UW's newspaper, *The Daily*, sponsored a song-writing contest with a $25 prize to the winner of the best fight song for an upcoming football game against the University of California. UW student **Lester Wilson** spent all night fine-tuning his song on the piano and won the contest. The Huskies also won the football game against the California Bears, 72–0, and the song was an instant hit with Husky fans.

"Bow down to Washington" has since been acclaimed as one of the most inspirational college fight songs ever written. UW students, alumni, and fans sing it proudly at Husky events.

"**Bow Down to Washington**"

Bow Down to Washington,
Bow Down to Washington,
Mighty Are The Men
Who Wear the Purple and the Gold,
Joyfully We Welcome Them
Within the Victors Fold.
We Will Carve Their Names
In the Hall of Fame
To Preserve the Memory of Our Devotion.
Heaven Help the Foes of Washington;

They're Trembling at the Feet
Of Mighty Washington,
The Boys Are There With Bells,
Their Fighting Blood Excels,
It's Harder to Push Them Over the Line
Than Pass the Dardanelles.
Victory the Cry of Washington...
Leather Lungs Together
With a Rah! Rah! Rah!
And O'er the Land
Our Loyal Band
Will Sing the Glory
Of Washington Forever.

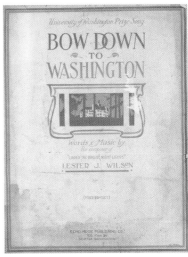

Lester Wilson's
Bow Down to Washington
sheet music, 1915.

Fast Fact: The lyrics to "Bow Down to Washington" have been changed many times throughout the years. The original lyrics mentioned the University of California mascot in verse two, "Bring the Golden Bear from his mighty lair" and "when we snare that Golden Bear, you'll never carry it back to California." These lines were later omitted as rivalries between other schools such as Washington State University and the University of Oregon intensified.

A contest entered just for fun,
Meant more than just some dollars won.
A tribute sung with such renown,
A victory cry that calls "Bow Down!"

is for Go Huskies!

The Husky Hall of Fame honors more than 200 of the greatest UW athletes and coaches since the school's athletics began to take shape in the 1890s. Here are just a few of those Husky sports legends.

Only two Husky basketball players have had their jerseys retired. Averaging nearly thirty-five points a game, consensus All-American **Bob Houbregs** helped his 1953 team to a third-place finish in the NCAA Final Four. Assisting with three straight NCAA Tournament appearances, **Brandon Roy** was named Pac-10 Player of the Year and first-team All-American for his 2005–2006 season.

Husky fans watched breathlessly as All-American pitcher **Danielle Lawrie** helped the UW women's softball team claim victory at the 2009 NCAA championship and a Pac-10 championship win the following year. In UW baseball, **Tim Lincecum** twice earned the Pac-10 Pitcher of the Year title. In 2006, he also won the Golden Spikes Award, which honors the best amateur player of the year. Playing for the San Francisco Giants, he helped his team win two World Series titles. **Courtney Thompson** helped lead her Husky volleyball team to its first NCAA championship in 2005. An Academic All-American, Courtney was also the first Husky to earn the prestigious Honda Award, presented to the top female athlete in the nation.

The Huskies have also had many outstanding coaches over the years. **Dorsett "Tubby" Graves** coached Husky baseball for twenty-four seasons and led his teams to win seven Northern Division titles between 1923 and 1946. With a coaching career spanning thirty-five years, **Clarence "Uncle Hec" Edmundson** not only coached record-breaking basketball teams, but led his track-and-field teams to seven Northwest Division titles and three Pacific Coast Conference championships. Named both a Pac-10 and NCAA Coach of the Year, **Marv Harshman** coached his teams to five post-season basketball tournament appearances from 1972 to 1985.

Danielle Lawrie, 2010.   *Tubby Graves, 1927.*   *Hec Edmundson, 1947.*

Fast Fact: It's all in the family for the Colellas! Because women's swimming was not yet a varsity sport at the UW in the early 1970s, Lynn Colella mostly practiced with the men's team. Her hard work paid off. She won the silver medal in the 200-meter butterfly at the 1972 Summer Olympics in Munich, becoming the UW's first female Olympic medalist. Not to be outdone by his sister, younger brother Rick Colella earned a bronze medal at the 1976 Summer Olympics in Montreal. Other siblings Steve and Pete Colella also competed for the UW swim team, both earning NCAA All-American titles.

From shooting hoops to running track,
Conference titles back to back.
Go, Dawgs! Be proud, be bold,
For the Purple and the Gold!

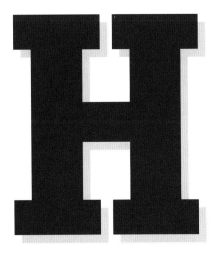

H is for Husky Football

Many Husky fans would agree—nothing ignites pride like a Husky football game. Here is a snapshot of a few of the award-winning players and coaches who've helped shape this remarkable program.

One of our greatest coaches in Husky football history is **Gilmour "Gloomy Gil" Dobie**. During his era as head coach from 1908 to 1916, the UW never lost a game. He coached **William "Wee" Coyle**, who was hailed as the "quarterback that never made a mistake" and also went unbeaten in his four seasons as a Husky.

During the 1920s, running back **Chuck Carroll** led the Husky charge with his passing, punting, and tackling. **George "Wildcat" Wilson** knocked opponents off their feet with his stiff-arm technique to avoid tackles. He led the Huskies to two Rose Bowls, in 1925 and 1926. In the 1950s, halfback **Hugh "the King" McElhenny** excited Husky fans by pulling off incredible offensive plays.

Coach **Jim Owens** took the reins in 1957. His underdog Huskies earned back-to-back Rose Bowl victories in 1960 and 1961 as well as the 1960 National Championship title. Running back and kicker **George Fleming** and quarterback **Bob Schloredt**, who had sight in just one eye, were team leaders and co-winners of the 1961 Rose Bowl Most Valuable Player Award. In 1963 and 1964, linebacker **Rick Redman** earned consensus All-American status. Quarterback **Alex**

"Sonny" Sixkiller helped rejuvenate Husky pride by leading the UW to a second-place Pac-8 finish in 1970.

Don James began his illustrious eighteen-year run as head coach during the 1970s, leading his teams to fifteen bowl games, four of which were Rose Bowl wins, and also the National Championship title in 1984. Helping usher in the new era of Husky football, quarterback **Warren Moon** led the Huskies to a 1978 Rose Bowl win, for which he was honored as Rose Bowl MVP. Defensive lineman and consensus All-American **Steve Emtman** helped the Huskies win Rose Bowls in 1990 and 1991 as well as the National Championship title in 1991. During this same era, and despite the lure of pro football, running back **Napoleon Kaufman** thrilled fans as one of UW's all-time leading rushers.

In early 2001, quarterback **Marques Tuiasosopo** launched Husky football into the new millennium with an 11–1 season record as well as a Rose Bowl win and MVP award. More recently, Coach **Steve Sarkisian**, along with a legion of talented players and loyal Husky fans, has continued the UW's football tradition of pride and excellence.

Fast Fact: Our Husky football legacy continues with the renovation of Husky Stadium completed in 2013. The oldest stadium in the Pac-12 Conference stands grander than ever—with a few changes. Premium seating and landscaped plazas are new, but some things will never change. Husky Stadium remains one of the loudest places to play college football!

Husky pride throughout the years—
Football greats, to you three cheers!
Excellence is our ambition.
Long live on our great tradition!

I is for In a House or In a Hall

Thousands of students attend the UW each year. Many of them live on or near the campus in apartments or homes, residence halls, or Greek houses.

Many freshmen start out campus life by living in a residence hall. In 1899, the first two dormitories were built, Lewis Hall for men and Clark Hall for women. The buildings remain but are no longer used for housing. Today there are many residence halls, which range from 1930s Tudor-style housing to sky-rise halls with stunning views of the Cascade Mountains and Lake Washington. On West Campus, the focus is on sustainability that includes energy and water-saving features. Many halls incorporate fitness centers.

The Greek housing community is well established on the north end of campus, where stately homes and lush trees line several streets and members share large residences. Many students decide to become a member in a fraternity (for men) or a sorority (for women) in hopes of creating a circle of close friends that may last a lifetime.

Letter initials from the Greek alphabet, such as gamma or delta, make up the names of fraternities or sororities. If students are "Greek," it usually means they are members in a house and are part of the Greek system.

Sigma Nu became the first fraternity on the UW campus in 1896. Chapters of Delta Gamma and Gamma Phi Beta, the first sororities on campus, were founded in the early 1900s. There are more than forty sororities and fraternities at the UW.

They encourage leadership and community service while also supporting academics.

Dorm life in 1942—the girls of Leary Hall.

Fast Fact: The FIJI fraternity boasts the most members on campus. The Sigma Alpha Epsilon fraternity has set itself apart by housing some of the most-beloved unofficial members of all. In 1922, the brothers adopted Frosty I, the first Husky mascot. The tradition has continued through the years, with a number of the UW's furry friends residing at the Sigma Alpha Epsilon house.

In a dorm or Greek house, too—
Huskies all, here at the U.
Working hard and gaining knowledge,
Friends for life you'll make in college.

J is for **Jacob Lawrence**

Huskies are surrounded by amazing professors who are experts in their fields. One of the most noted and cherished faculty members of the UW was artist **Jacob Lawrence**.

When Jacob was a young boy, he enjoyed catching insects, and he soon began sketching the bugs he spotted. When Jacob was thirteen, he moved to Harlem in New York City with his family. Won over by the energy of the city, he soaked up the sights, sounds, and smells of his new home. He also delighted in exploring his neighborhood's busy streets. Jacob imagined that each doorway, window, or building told a unique and interesting story. Trying to keep Jacob busy, his mother signed him up for an after-school program. During those sessions, he experimented with various art materials as he re-created impressions of the world around him in the art he created. As Jacob learned about black history, heroes, and art, he was inspired to express his discoveries through his paintings.

Although Jacob became discouraged that it might be difficult to make a living as an artist, he continued working hard at his paintings. People began to see his special talent reflected in his artwork, and supporters helped him show his pieces in respected galleries beyond Harlem. As his paintings of famous black heroes were praised, African Americans took pride that an accomplished artist was highlighting their accomplishments. Jacob experienced great success as an artist for many years. He went on to share his talent and support students in developing their artistic abilities. Jacob taught art at the UW from 1971 until 1985. He has won numerous prestigious awards, including the Washington State Governor's Award and the National Medal of Arts.

Creating another masterpiece! Artist and UW faculty member, Jacob Lawrence, hard at work, 1979.

Fast Fact: When Jacob wanted to tell a story using a series of paintings, he would work on all the paintings at once, using one color at a time. He believed his story flowed more smoothly when he used the same colors on each painting in a series. Some of his series of paintings consisted of more than forty scenes that were painted color by color.

Stories of freedom and of fear,
His paintings spoke loud and clear.
Wowing crowds across the nation,
He became a huge sensation!

K is for Kane Hall

Imagine sitting in a large auditorium amid a crowd of students eagerly taking notes on a professor's lecture. That's what often comes to mind when a Husky remembers **Kane Hall**.

Most students enter college knowing their general interests but have not yet narrowed their academic focus. The large lecture rooms on campus, such as those in Kane Hall, make it possible for students to venture out to learn something new.

Constructed in 1970, Kane Hall sits on the northern edge of Red Square. The prominent lecture hall hosts rooms of many sizes that are used primarily for university classes. Its largest auditorium holds more than seven hundred people. UW students are not the only ones who benefit from the grand halls. Kane also accommodates events including town hall meetings and worship services as well as an occasional movie. Committed to providing enriching forums to the public, Kane Hall has welcomed many renowned speakers over the years.

Kane Hall was named after **Thomas Franklin Kane**, who served as UW's president from 1902 to 1914. He is recognized for rapidly increasing the university's enrollment from about 600 students to more than 2,800. Faculty numbers also increased during those years. Doctorate degrees were common among the staffers, which made it possible for the university to increase its specialized courses and advanced programs. The changes helped the UW grow into an even more established university.

UW President Thomas Kane, early 1900s.

Fast Fact: Appreciated by many, the History Lecture Series is an annual tradition in Kane Hall. The lecture series started in a unique way. A state law at the time did not allow professors older than age seventy to teach. When beloved history professor Giovanni Costigan retired in 1975, he continued to lecture for years as a guest speaker by invitation of the UW Alumni Association.

Taking notes inside Kane Hall,
Among many, one and all.
Students past came here to learn.
Now a Husky, it's your turn!

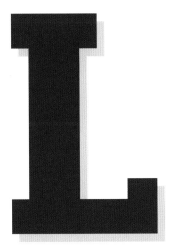

L is for **Libraries**

When you attend the UW, you will experience many aspects of college life, especially studying for classes. The UW Libraries are part of a leading research institution and are home to the largest collection of research materials in the Pacific Northwest.

The grand and elegant Suzzallo Library is among the most memorable sites you'll see on campus. **Henry Suzzallo** became president of the UW in 1915. One of his first goals was to build a beautiful, fully equipped library for students. He spoke of the UW as the "University of a Thousand Years" and believed that the library he envisioned should be a campus monument that would be the soul of the university. In 1933, the library was named in his honor.

Suzzallo Library is indeed a monument, with its impressive Gothic arches and spires. Its Reading Room has been praised as the most beautiful in North America, a quiet study room with stunning glass windows, hand-carved wood, and soaring ceilings. It's so quiet at times that you'll want to grasp your books tightly. A pin drop could possibly echo, not to mention a tumbling binder.

Odegaard Undergraduate Library is named for **Charles E. Odegaard**, who became UW president in 1958. It is known for its group study rooms and large technology lab. Some UW libraries focus on specific areas of study, including the Engineering Library, the Foster Business Library, and the Music Library.

Allen Library was built in 1990. Its name honors **Kenneth Allen**, who served as an associate director for UW Libraries for more than twenty years—and who is the father of Microsoft cofounder Paul Allen.

The mission of the UW libraries is to connect people with knowledge and to help all Husky students succeed through this knowledge and discovery.

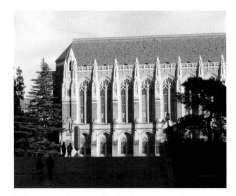

The grand Suzzallo Library, 2013.

Beloved Huskies, Professor Edmond Meany and UW President, Henry Suzzallo, 1920.

Fast Fact: The eighteen figures atop the Suzzallo Library were sculpted by Allan Clark. They represent luminaries who have contributed to world culture and learning, including playwright William Shakespeare, artist and inventor Leonardo da Vinci, and the great American Benjamin Franklin.

Walk on campus, find its soul,
You'll end up at Suzzallo.
Here you'll study with your peers
At the "U of a Thousand Years"!

M is for **Minoru Yamasaki**

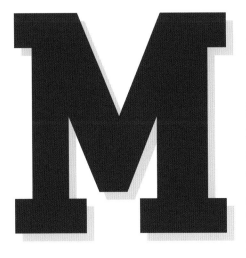

Detroit, New York, and Seattle have something impressive in common—skylines that are graced with the vision of UW graduate and famed architect, **Minoru Yamasaki**. He believed that modern buildings could be beautiful and peaceful as well as functional.

Minoru, whose parents emigrated from Japan, was born in Seattle in 1912. He grew up poor but was a bright student who excelled in science and math. When Minoru was in high school, his visiting uncle shared some of his architectural drawings. That moment sparked Minoru's strong desire to become an architect, which in turn inspired him to enroll at the University of Washington.

To help pay for college expenses, Minoru spent several summers working in fish canneries in Alaska. There, he faced miserable conditions, long hours, and racial prejudice. School was a challenge at times, but Minoru received encouragement from a professor who predicted he would become one of the best architects to graduate from the UW. Minoru's hard work and dedication to his dream soon turned that prediction into reality. After graduating in 1934, he moved to New York and worked in several architectural firms. Many years later, he moved to Detroit, Michigan, and opened his own firm. He vowed to always treat his employees with fairness and respect.

Minoru designed countless buildings and other structures in his lifetime, which include peaceful fountains and classic archways. He believed that the beauty of classic architecture could be present in modern buildings made by machines. Minoru's architectural fingerprints are evident in cities throughout the world. His hometown of Seattle boasts his creations including the Pacific Science Center and the Rainier Bank Tower. A true Husky legend, Minoru was honored with the Alumni Summa Laude Dignatus Award in 1960.

Minoru Yamasaki, with one of his models, 1950s.

Fast Fact: One of the most prominent architects of the twentieth century, Minoru was featured on the cover of TIME magazine on January 18, 1963. His firm's many designs include the twin towers of the World Trade Center in New York City, which were completed in 1976. The towers were part of New York City's world-renowned skyline for more than twenty-five years, until their destruction in the devastating terrorist attack on September 11, 2001.

New York, Detroit, Seattle, too,
Boast the works of Minoru.
Skylines that can touch a cloud,
This UW legend makes us proud.

PACIFIC SCIENCE CENTER

N is for Natural History

Banana slugs and nuthatches may sound like fictitious creatures, but the bright yellow slugs and the small birds live in the Pacific Northwest. In the winter of 1879, a group of young men in Seattle formed a club to learn about animals that inhabit the region. The club evolved into a group devoted to the study of natural history. The members collected specimens including shells and birds, and gave presentations about what they'd discovered and learned. In 1885, they decided to officially call themselves the Young Naturalists. As more members joined, including university professors, the group earned respect as an established society. Its growing collections were used to teach students and were traded with other natural history societies throughout the United States. Who could have imagined that the first museum in the state of Washington would owe its early beginnings to a few young men who were curious about nature and loved to learn?

The Burke Museum of Natural History and Culture, or simply the Burke, as students call it, is a popular spot for all Seattleites. It houses some of the most impressive collections of Native American artifacts in the world. At the Burke, you can find a broad range of interesting items, from intricate Chinook baskets to colorful Haida bird masks. If you're curious about the biology of birds, you'll have a field day at the Burke. It houses one of the largest ornithology collections in the world. If you like learning about dinosaurs and past life forms, then you will appreciate the Burke's resources that focus on paleontology, including a replica of a dinosaur near the entrance.

Check out the Burke next time you're on campus. The beloved Seattle museum has come a long way from that simple idea the four Young Naturalists cooked up on a cold winter's day more than 130 years ago.

The four Young Naturalist Society founders, 1882.

Tsimshian Memorial Pole and Haida House Front Pole, 2013.

Fast Fact: Why is the museum called the Burke? Originally called the Washington State Museum, it was renamed in 1962 for pioneer and judge, Thomas Burke, a chief justice of the Washington State Supreme Court in the late 1800s. He and his wife Caroline loved Native Americans and their history and collected many artifacts. Caroline honored her husband's wishes that his estate was to be used to promote a better understanding of the people of the Pacific Northwest—and it did by helping fund the Burke.

Let there be no mystery
With Pacific Northwest history.
Tribal artifacts you'll find,
Treasures that were left behind.

O is for Old Traditions

With a history as old and fascinating as the UW's, it's not surprising that some unique traditions have been established over the years. Here are a few of the traditions that help make the University of Washington special.

The Denny Bell: Carried by wagon from the old Territorial UW campus in downtown Seattle to its current home atop Denny Hall, the Denny Bell was first rung in 1862 to signal the start of classes. Throughout history, it announced some important events such as the death of Abraham Lincoln in 1865, the Great Seattle Fire in 1889, and President Kennedy's visit to the UW in 1961. It is now rung annually to mark the UW's homecoming game.

The Sacred Hook: Between 1908 and 1916, the UW football team, under the direction of Coach Gil Dobie, was undefeated. A symbol of Husky dominance, the Hook was unveiled in 1911—mimicking the idea taken from the old vaudeville acts that yanked people from the stage if they weren't performing well. The Hook was used to rattle the nerves of the opposing team. The current whereabouts of the Hook is unknown, but the legend lives on.

Husky Spirit Traditions: Many Husky fans will argue that the famous fan "wave," began at the UW. In 1981, Husky band leader **Bill Bissell** and yell king **Robb Weller** began leading crowds of Husky football fans to stand and sit at games, creating a wavelike motion of people around the stadium. Bissell is also credited with adding two songs, "Tequila" and "Louie Louie" to the UW band's playlist. Since 1921, the Siren is heard when the UW football team enters the field, scores, or wins.

Husky Tailgating: Since the 1920s, many Husky fans have enjoyed a tradition that is unique to the UW. Sailgating is a term coined by pregame enthusiasts that reinvents tailgating for fans. They sailgate by celebrating with family and friends aboard boats moored just off the shores of Husky Stadium in Union Bay.

Husky fans march onto Denny Field with the Sacred Hook, circa 1913.

Fast Fact: In 1909, a group of UW sophomores decided to teach some freshmen who was "the boss." Captured then marched to what was then known as the Geyser Basin—they were tossed in the water. A tradition was born that day, and the Geyser Basin, that you might know as Drumheller Fountain, has been nicknamed Frosh Pond ever since.

Every Husky understands
Our cheering goes beyond the stands.
When other fans are tailgating,
We're on the lake and sailgating!

P is for Publications

How do Husky students, staff members, and alumni know what's happening on campus? The university produces several publications to keep Dawg fans informed of daily life and events at the UW.

As its name suggests, *The Daily*, UW's independent student-run newspaper, is printed every weekday when school is in session. It is a trusted source for timely news. *The Daily's* mission is "to serve the UW campus community by producing the most fair and balanced newspaper possible." Reaching nearly 65,000 students and staff online or through the 10,000 copies printed daily, it has one of the largest circulations in the Seattle area .

First published in 1891, the paper had various names in its early years, including the *Pacific Wave*, the *College Idea*, and the *University of Washington Daily*. It has been called *The Daily* since 1976. The paper has won numerous awards and is a nationally recognized publication.

Columns magazine primarily targets Husky graduates and is written by the staff of the UW Alumni Association. It shares news and highlights about the university and its people. The quarterly magazine began in 1908 as the *Washington Alumnus* and has a circulation of approximately 220,000. It is one of the top five consumer magazines in the Puget Sound area and is among the finest award-winning university magazines in the nation.

UW's first yearbook, the *Tyee*, was published in 1900 and dedicated to the graduating class of 1901. Written by members of the junior class until 1912, the Associated Students of the UW took over and published the *Tyee* for years. It was published with some interruptions from the early '70s to the '80s, and publication ceased altogether in 1994. Copies of the *Tyee* have become some of the most-requested items from the UW's Special Collections because they preserve Husky memories from years past.

Bringing the news to students in hardworking Husky fashion, 1938.

Fast Fact: Before becoming a reporter for The Daily, a student must first apply for Daily 101. The ten-week trial helps new writers become more proficient journalists. Two of the UW's most well-known cartoonists, David Horsey ('76) and Mike Luckovich ('82) began their careers at The Daily. Both went on to twice win the Pulitzer Prize for editorial cartooning, making Huskies everywhere proud.

Stories, sports, and UW news,
Articles with student views.
Staffed by students—then and now,
Husky writers, take a bow!

is for the **Quad**

Come late March or early April, the most scenic place on the UW campus is the Liberal Arts Quadrangle, or "the Quad." Each spring the pink burst of cherry tree blossoms, set against the green grass and red pathways of terracotta bricks, creates a fairyland of color.

Surrounded by ornate collegiate Gothic-style buildings, the Quad was designed in 1915 by **Carl Gould**, a local architect and UW professor. For its first seventy years, the Quad was an open, muddy, and often unused field. It was so underused that the campus Reserved Officers' Training Corps, or ROTC, used it for marching drills.

It wasn't until the 1960s that architect **Fred Mann** had the brilliant idea to fill the empty space on the Quad. The Washington Park Arboretum, which cultivates a unique collection of plants and trees from around the world, was in the midst of a highway construction project. A large number of Yoshino cherry trees were about to be destroyed. With the support of UW President Charles Odegaard and landscape architect **Eric Hoyte**, arborists successfully relocated more than three hundred trees to the UW campus. Thirty of those trees continue to grow and blossom in the Quad, helping to elegantly frame the wide-open space.

The Quad remains a wondrous place on campus. No matter the season, the beauty of the classic architecture, the layout of the pathways, and the magic of the cherry trees make it a favorite sanctuary for students, faculty, and visitors alike.

Students at the Quad, Campus Day, 1929.

The iconic cherry blossoms in the Quad, 2012.

Fast Fact: In April 1962, in an effort to save money, UW officials were planning to replace sections of the Quad's brickwork with black asphalt. Students protested this "blackening of the Quad" by signing petitions and holding rallies. President Odegaard and his staff found the funds needed to re-lay new brick on the pathways. Although it took a number of years to complete the work, the Quad ultimately kept its brick pathways, thanks to the voices of many UW students!

A campus planned with lots of care,
All Husky students proudly share.
No greater beauty will you find—
Our cherry blooms are one of a kind!

R is for Red Square

When most people hear references to **Red Square**, they might first envision the Red Square in Moscow, Russia. However, any Husky who hears a mention of Red Square is more likely to become lost in memories of hanging out in the sun or participating in pep rallies or witnessing protests.

UW's Red Square serves many functions. Campus legend has it that slippery red bricks were used to construct the plaza in an effort to discourage large protests. In actuality, it was thought that our campus already had many open green spaces, so a large gathering place was needed. Officially known as Central Plaza, Red Square was completed in 1971, with thousands of bricks having been laid. The plaza was designed by **Paul Hayden Kirk**, a UW graduate and prominent Pacific Northwest architect, and its main purpose was to provide a roof for a 1,000-car underground garage. Visitors have access to many buildings on the main campus from the garage, which helps keep them dry on rainy days. Paul also designed **Meany Hall** and the **Odegaard Undergraduate Library**, both near Red Square.

The three brick towers that flank Red Square are not only impressive visually but also serve a purpose. One of the towers ventilates the parking garage below. But after that tower was constructed, many felt that having just one structure took away from the grandeur of Red Square. Two more towers were constructed to make the overall design more pleasing to the eye. Red Square also incorporates one of the most expensive pieces of art in the state, **Barnett Newman's** sculpture "Broken Obelisk" that weighs more than two tons.

Built during the height of the Vietnam War, UW's Red Square quickly became a place where students could convene to protest and voice opinions. It continues to be a popular gathering place and main thoroughfare for thousands of students each day.

Construction in Red Square leaves the "excecutive swimming pool", 1969.

"Broken Obelisk" in Red Square, 2012.

Fast Fact: During the 1969 construction of several buildings adjacent to Red Square, there was for a time nothing but an enormous pit in the space where the plaza exists today. Many UW staffers remember references to the hole as the "executive swimming pool."

Paved to be a gathering place,
A sea of red, wide-open space,
A place to relax, a thoroughfare—
We'll always remember you, Red Square.

 **is for Seattle**

The Emerald City and the University of Washington have grown up together. With the village of Seattle established in 1851, and the birth of the Territorial University just ten years later, these siblings of sorts are linked with an amazing history that spans more than 150 years. Here are a few reasons that make it so easy to love Seattle.

The Great Outdoors: Surrounded by the Puget Sound, lakes, and mountains, UW students are in for a true Pacific Northwest experience. A boating haven, Seattle offers many water activities, such as kayaking, sailing, and riding aboard ferry boats. Students might even get to live on a houseboat! With the Cascades to the east, the Olympics to the west, and Mount Rainier to the south, the outdoor experiences are impressive—and endless. A day trip might include a hike in a nearby rain forest or whale watching in the San Juan Islands. Picnic along Lake Washington, or if you ski, head up to Crystal Mountain.

Pike Place Market: Dating back to 1907, Seattle's Pike Place Market is a hub for locals and visitors alike. With farmers selling fresh foods, fish mongers throwing fish, craftspeople selling their wares, and street performers and musicians entertaining the crowds, the market is truly a colorful experience.

Iconic Seattle: The most iconic structure and cherished landmark in all of Seattle may be the **Space Needle**. Built for the 1962 futuristic-themed Century 21 Exposition, it offers a breathtaking bird's eye view of the city. Known for its unique architectural design, the Experience Music Project, or **EMP**, is a museum dedicated to the history and exploration of music, science fiction, and pop culture. Once a coal bunker and gas processing plant, **Gas Works Park** is perched along scenic Lake Union, where it proudly displays its industrial roots among green, grassy hills.

Huskies love their city and living in Seattle is one of the best perks of attending the UW.

Seattle's Pike Place Market, 1919.

Fast Fact: What lives under Seattle's Aurora Bridge? Why it's the Fremont Troll! This eighteen-foot-high sculpture—complete with shaggy hair, one enormous hubcap eye, and a Volkswagen Beetle in his giant grasp—has charmed residents and visitors alike since 1990.

With crystal lakes and mountains high,
A spacelike needle scrapes the sky—
You are beloved, ever true,
Emerald City, we love you.

T is for Territorial University

The UW campus is beautifully spread out on the shores of Union and Portage Bays, but did you ever wonder where it all began? Its roots reach a few miles to downtown Seattle... In 1861, twenty-eight years before Washington became a state, settlers hoped to build an institution of higher learning, a university, in the young village of Seattle. That vision would eventually grow into our treasured University of Washington.

Two men who worked tirelessly together were key in turning the dream into a reality. **Arthur Denny**, one of the first settlers in Seattle, donated some of his own land and convinced others to do the same. Reverend **Daniel Bagley** took care of the business side and recruited volunteers to clear the forested land.

On September 16, 1861, the Territorial University was born—and classes began on November 4 that year. **Asa Mercer**, became the university's first president and instructor. As the city grew, the university did, too. It soon became clear that the original ten acres was not enough land to support a growing university. Washington became a state in November 1889, with its new dreams, new leaders, and new plans. The university found a new leader soon after that in **Edmond Meany**, a member of the Washington Legislature. Edmond, who graduated from the university in 1885, helped make the purchase of the current site possible. In 1895, the UW moved to the new campus from which it has proudly stood ever since.

Seattle pioneer and UW founder, Arthur Denny, 1890s.

Reverend Daniel Bagley, UW founder, 1860s.

The four columns, 1922.

Fast Fact: You will find reminders of UW's rich history all around the campus. One of the first buildings of the Territorial University included an elegant two-story structure supported by four stately columns. Those columns were transported to the current campus and stand today in front of Sylvan Theater. They symbolize loyalty, industry, faith, and efficiency, with the first letter of each word spelling the word "life." Meany, Denny, and Bagley Halls are named after these great men and ambitious founders.

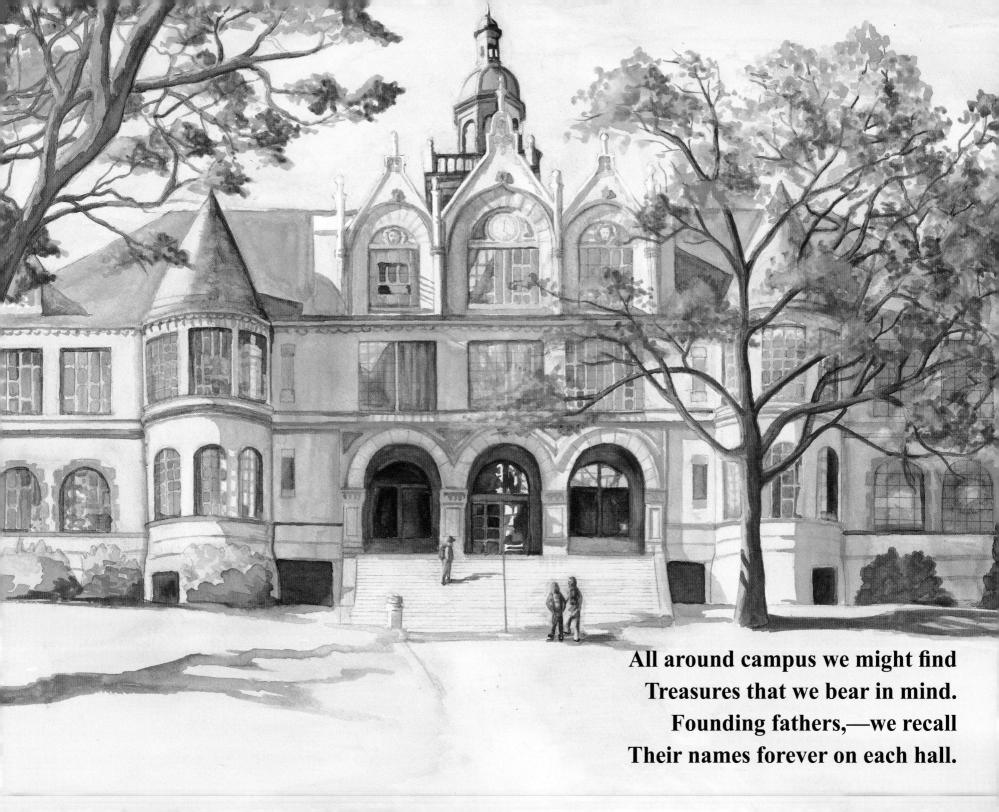

All around campus we might find
Treasures that we bear in mind.
Founding fathers,—we recall
Their names forever on each hall.

U is for **UW Medicine**

The city of Seattle is renowned for its cutting-edge medical community and research. That is in large part because of the UW's medical program and the many alumni who have done groundbreaking work in the areas of medicine and science. Here are just a few of the brilliant alumni who have benefited the world with their life's work and have been honored by the UW with the Alumnus Summa Laude Dignatus Award.

After losing his brother, baseball great Fred Hutchinson, to cancer in 1964, UW alumnus **William Hutchinson** dreamed of an organization that would fund researching physicians. That dream was realized in 1975 with the opening of the Fred Hutchinson Cancer Research Center in Seattle. The center is an international leader in the pursuit of cancer prevention and treatments.

After receiving his PhD in biochemistry at UW in 1954, **Martin Rodbell** made an important discovery. He discovered how G proteins help cells in the body communicate with one another. The discovery earned him the Nobel Prize in Medicine in 1994.

A UW medical school graduate, **William Foege** became one of the foremost leaders in the global health community. He served as the director of the US Centers for Disease Control and is most widely recognized for his work with the smallpox disease. In the 1970s his strategy to eradicate smallpox helped save countless lives worldwide.

Wayne Quinton is often heralded as the pioneer of bio-engineering, a field that combines engineering and medicine. His groundbreaking work included designs for more than forty medical devices and lifesaving procedures.

Young college lads before they knew how many millions of lives they would save with their medical contributions, Wayne Quinton (left), 1940 and William Foege (right), 1961.

Fast Fact: Curious about the way things work from a young age, Wayne Quinton was recruited by Boeing at the start of World War II. He held a number of jobs with the company and worked on its B-29 bomber. In 1949, Quinton switched his focus to medicine when he began his work at the UW, improving existing medical equipment and creating new devices. In the university's medical shop, Quinton was part of the team that created the lifesaving shunt for kidney patients, which has saved millions of lives. He also invented the modern light-weight treadmill.

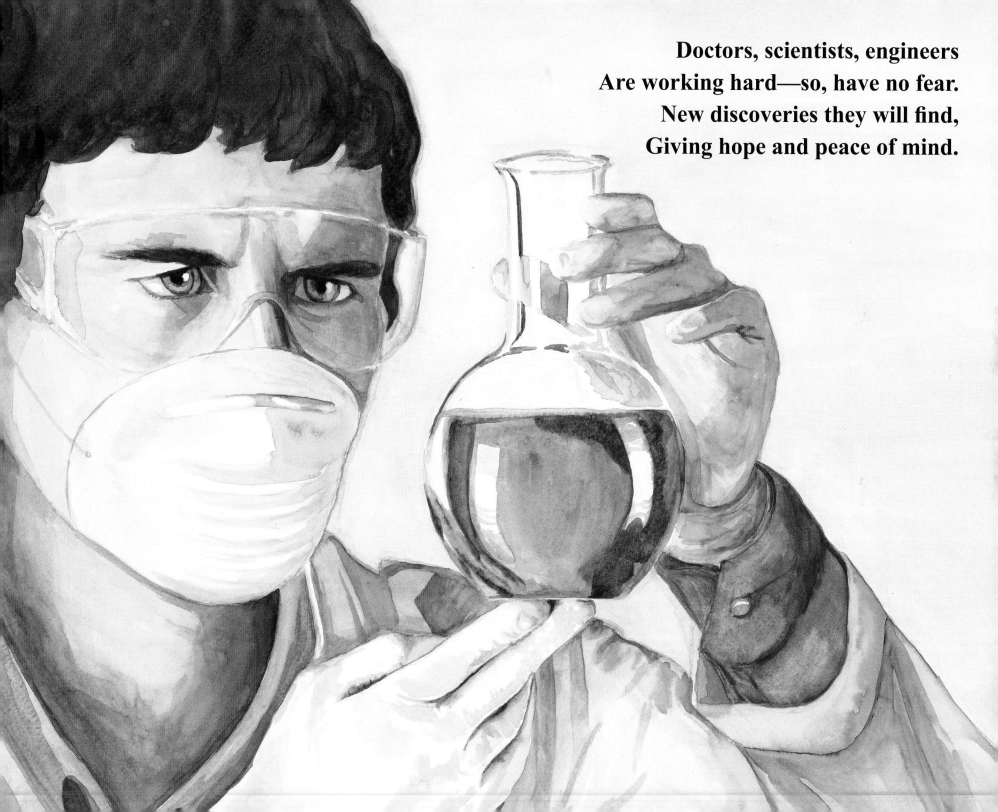

Doctors, scientists, engineers
Are working hard—so, have no fear.
New discoveries they will find,
Giving hope and peace of mind.

V is for Vistas

Imagine walking on campus one cool misty morning and heading to class. Slowly the mist begins to clear. As you head toward **Drumheller Fountain**, you might peer through a blizzard of pink cherry blossoms to catch a glimpse of the majestic snow-covered peak of Mount Rainier rising skyward. Rays of sunlight reveal a beauty that can't be ignored. The path you take toward the fountain is perfectly aligned with this amazing vista. Breathtaking views appear from various vantage points on the University of Washington campus.

The original designers of the UW were well aware of the natural beauty of the site. They understood the university was located in a spectacularly picturesque place. To emphasize the beauty, they created walkways and buildings in specific areas that aligned with these natural vistas. These designers, the celebrated **Olmsted Brothers**, created a plan for the UW campus that has been preserved to this day. Their solid reputation reached from coast to coast. For the A-Y-P, they designed the walkway leading directly towards Mount Rainier, called **Rainier Vista**. More than a hundred years ago, Edmond Meany said, "No campus in all the world can equal Rainier Vista."

This vista is still the centerpiece of the campus today. Views of Lake Washington, the Cascade Mountains, Portage Bay, the Olympic Mountains, and Lake Union can also be seen from campus. Throughout the years with additional construction of various buildings, some of the original vistas have disappeared. However, a few remain that will continue to inspire students, faculty, and visitors for generations to come.

A stunning sunset vista with the George Washington statue silhouetted against the Olympic Mountains, 2011.

Fast Fact: A mountain that plays peek-a-boo? Anyone who is new to Seattle, or just visiting, may have little sense of just how close Mount Rainier is. But any uncertainty about the mountain's proximity disappears the first day the clouds clear and it appears in all its glory. Who knows? Mount Rainier may have been hiding in cloud cover when the Olmsted brothers first visited the campus in 1904. In their initial designs, there was no mention of Mount Rainier. When they returned in 1906 to design plans for the A-Y-P, Mount Rainier became the centerpiece of the entire campus. Huskies love the Rainier Vista. Its beauty and majesty are unforgettable.

Beyond the pathway, toward the fountain,
Rises our majestic mountain.
A tall fir, a cherry blossom,
Make this sacred vista awesome!

W is for **William H. Gates Hall**

Courtroom drama has always been a popular theme in both television and film. Actors dramatize courtroom scenes, but in real life, people often call on attorneys for situations in which expert advice about the law is needed. At some point in your life, you might call on a lawyer to help you. Lawyers interpret the law and advise people about their rights. Laws can be very complicated, and lawyers play an important role in society.

Established in 1899, the UW School of Law opened with two rooms at the Territorial University. As it expanded, the Law School relocated several times. Today, the William H. Gates Hall is home to the UW School of Law and is one of the most impressive glass buildings on campus. Built in 2003, it offers students the latest interactive media and technology and is named after UW School of Law alumnus **William H. Gates Sr.**

Born is Bremerton, Washington, William is no stranger to public service. While still enrolled in college, he served three years in the US Army during World War II. He graduated from the UW School of Law in 1950. With his degree in hand, William soon became a partner in a business law firm in Seattle. As president of the Washington State Bar Association, the father of three, and a lawyer, he still found time to serve both the local and global communities. He is the founder of the Initiative for Global Development, through which business leaders around the globe work together to end poverty. In 1991, he earned the UW School of Law Distinguished Alumnus Award, and he honors the UW as a true civic leader.

William H. Gates Hall, 2013.

Fast Fact: Serving one's community is important to the Gates family. William's first wife, Mary, is remembered as a leader who firmly believed in promoting education, volunteer service, and philanthropy. Named in her honor, Mary Gates Hall on the UW campus is the center for undergraduate learning. The Mary Gates Endowment attracts and supports undergraduate students in their research and studies. William and Mary's son, Bill Gates, cofounder of Microsoft, strives to end poor health and poverty through the Bill and Melinda Gates Foundation.

Serve your community, help those in need.
William and Mary have done that indeed.
To know the law is another way
Attorneys serve our world today.

X is for eXcellence

Whether you play sports or do well at school, doing your best just feels great. When you become a Husky, you are in good company with many professors and students who strive for excellence.

One way Huskies show excellence is to help others. The School of Nursing is just one example of the university's many remarkable programs. U.S. News & World Report magazine has ranked it as the number one nursing school in the nation for more than twenty-five years. The UW also has highly reputable schools of medicine and dentistry.

Considered a public research school, the UW receives government funds to conduct its many studies. One exciting project conducted by the School of Environmental and Forest Sciences is the development of biofuel—a fuel made from plant materials. Nationally acclaimed, the school has been recognized as one the top three forest science graduate schools in the US.

Those who enjoy working with students and children will find equally rewarding paths to follow at the UW. Innovative programs and great community partnerships are two reasons why the UW School of Education is consistently ranked as one of the top education schools in the nation. Teachers who earn their degree at the UW are in a class of their own.

The UW's commitment to excellence is widespread. It's possible to be a Husky even for those who don't live near the Seattle campus. Founded in 1990, the UW sister branch campuses in Bothell and Tacoma make it possible for students in nearby cities and counties to access UW excellence in higher learning.

Whichever campus you attend and whichever field of study you choose, as a Husky, you can count on an excellent education that will open doors to a bright future. Excellence is a proud UW tradition.

Proud graduates showing their Husky pride, Commencement, 2012.

Fast Fact: Some students in the UW's Foster School of Business have the opportunity to climb Mt. Rainier, one of the highest mountains in the US. Making the challenging climb not only helps them learn leadership skills that are practical in business but also enables them to raise funds for nonprofit organizations like the Boys & Girls Clubs and the Special Olympics. Now that is truly excellent!

Working hard to do your best,
In your future you'll invest.
Ask all around, it's agreed—
UW grads will surely lead!

Y is for **Yearly Rivalries**

The bright fall leaves and cool crisp air can mean only one thing on the UW campus—Husky football season has arrived! Each year, Husky fans check their game schedule for a few key games, including the Oregon matchup and the Apple Cup.

The rivalry between the UW and the University of Oregon Ducks, known as the Border War, dates back to the early 1900s. Husky coach Gil Dobie had never lost a game, and in 1916, with both the UW and Oregon holding perfect season records, the long-awaited matchup offered no clear winner—it was a tie game. Although the Huskies were crowned the Pacific Coast Conference champions, the Oregon Ducks played in the Rose Bowl that year, because it was cheaper for them to travel to the game in California. Thus began a spirited rivalry, which has intensified over the years.

Toward the end of each football season, the Huskies play against another rival, the Washington State Cougars, in the Apple Cup game. Since 1900, these in-state rivals have faced off almost every year. The Apple Cup trophy is proudly displayed on the winning team's campus for an entire year—motivating the opposing team to win it back at the next Apple Cup.

One of the most memorable Husky victories was the 1975 Apple Cup. The UW had been trailing when Husky **Alvin Burleson** returned an interception with a record-breaking

ninety-three yards for a touchdown! Thus began one the greatest comebacks in the UW's history. The Huskies went on to win the game by a score of 28–27, and the win helped Coach Don James earn a place in the hearts of all Dawg fans.

Huskies look forward to the Apple Cup and Border War games each year. Fans of each team seize the opportunity to bask in victory while razzing friends who are fans of the opposing team. Each highly anticipated game is remembered and analyzed for years to come.

An early Apple Cup rally depicting this great rivalry, 1912.

UW coaching legend Gil Dobie, 1911.

Fast Fact: In 1911, just as the Border War with the Oregon Ducks was heating up, legendary Husky quarterback Wee Coyle tricked the Oregon players in a surprising way. By pretending that his leather helmet was actually the football, he distracted the Ducks while another UW player ran the real ball in for a touchdown. The Huskies won the game 29-3, and the trick play became known as the Dobie Bunk Play in recognition of Coach Gil Dobie.

Every Husky waits all year
For rival games—we're here to cheer.
Husky wins mean bragging rights.
Go Purple and Gold! Fight, Dawgs, fight!

Z is for **Zoology**

Zoology is the study of animals, and it helps us understand wildlife and the environment. **Shirley Malcom** and **Jane Lubchenco** are two noted zoologists who studied at the University of Washington and Alumnus Summa Laude Dignatus Award recipients.

Shirley Malcom worked hard becoming a top student in her high school. She enrolled at the UW in 1963. During her freshman year, she struggled in some of her science classes. She was also often the only woman in those classes—and many times, she was also the only African American student. Despite the challenges, she never gave up. She continued to believe in herself and sought help when she needed it. In 1967, she was one of the first women to graduate with a BS in zoology from the UW. She has served in leadership positions at the American Association for the Advancement of Science. In these roles, she has supported science education for women and minority students who might not otherwise have had the opportunity to pursue scientific studies. This has been one of her greatest accomplishments.

Jane Lubchenco chose the University of Washington for graduate school because of its stellar marine biology and ecology programs. She earned a master's degree in zoology in 1971. Jane's main research project was to carefully study the eating habits of two types of sea stars along the rocky shorelines of the Pacific Northwest. Her work has been instrumental in solving real-world problems such as how pollution affects organisms or how oxygen-poor water affects the Dungeness crab. Jane has written many highly regarded papers in marine ecology and has become an accomplished marine scientist. Her writings are referenced throughout the world. She also became the first woman to head the National Oceanic and Atmospheric Administration.

Both of these women are admired Huskies and zoologists who have used their education to benefit the world.

Shirley M. Malcom, 2005.

Jane Lubchenco, 2009.

Fast Fact: Zoologists study many kinds of animals—even butterflies. An extensive fire in the UW's zoology laboratory in 1997 almost ruined decades' worth of research on butterflies. It took approximately forty to fifty firefighters to put it out. Even though years' worth of data was lost, far more research would have been destroyed if not for a thick fire door and the determination of the firefighters.